Exploring the Moon

By Suzanne Weyn
Illustrated by Tom McKee

Scott Foresman
is an imprint of

Glenview, Illinois • Boston, Massachusetts • Chandler, Arizona •
Upper Saddle River, New Jersey

Illustrations

Tom McKee.

Photographs

Every effort has been made to secure permission and provide appropriate credit for photographic material. The publisher deeply regrets any omission and pledges to correct errors called to its attention in subsequent editions.

Unless otherwise acknowledged, all photographs are the property of Pearson Education, Inc.

22 NASA.

ISBN 13: 978-0-328-51632-2
ISBN 10:   0-328-51632-5

1 2 3 4 5 6 7 8 9 10 V0G1 13 12 11 10 09

Cathy searched the skies above Shining Lake but saw nothing unusual. Deep down, she knew she wouldn't. Cathy had only hoped to catch a bit of yellow streaking across the sky—anything at all to make her feel part of this historic day.

It was Wednesday, July 16, 1969. That morning, the United States had launched a giant Saturn V rocket into space. Its mission was to send three men into outer space.

The space mission was called Apollo 11. The astronauts onboard had important goals. They would walk on the moon, make observations, collect samples of rocks and soil, and return home. It would be the first time in history that anyone had ever done this.

Cathy was interested in everything about space travel. She had read about all the earlier missions that had led to this one. She had marked the day of the Moon landing and walk on her calendar. Then the most awful thing had happened. Cathy's parents had insisted on sending her to summer camp!

"I can't go then," Cathy had protested. "The Moon walk is during those weeks. I can't miss being home for that. That camp has no TVs. I need to see the Moon walk on TV."

"Those are the only weeks the camp had open," her father said. "You need to get outside more, see nature."

"You'll meet other kids your age," Cathy's mother added. "You spend too much time here with us."

"I don't want to get outside and see nature. I don't want to meet kids. I want to see the Moon walk," Cathy insisted.

It hadn't mattered. She wound up at Camp Shining Lake just the same. Cathy knew her parents meant well. They just wanted her to have more friends. The truth was that Cathy would much rather read about space and space travel than do anything else. Her parents just didn't understand. Nobody did.

Cathy continued looking up for signs of the rocket until a counselor told her that free swim was over. It was time for lunch. Moving slowly, Cathy changed in her cabin and headed for the camp mess hall by herself.

Cathy often felt lonely at camp. Most of the other campers already knew each other from previous summers. Cathy found it hard to join a group of campers she didn't know. Meals were the worst times. Mostly she just ate quietly while the others talked and laughed around her.

Once in a while Cathy imagined herself attempting to join in a conversation. She wondered what would happen if she just spoke up or asked a question. Probably no words would come out of her mouth or maybe worse, she would say something stupid. Then the girls would just laugh at her, and it would make her feel embarrassed. No, it was just easier and safer to keep to herself. Not having friends wasn't such a big deal.

For the last three nights, Camp Shining Lake had built campfires. Sometimes a counselor would tell a scary story. Some of the stories were so terrifying that they made the campers scream and huddle closer together. The stories didn't frighten Cathy though because she wasn't paying attention.

Instead she would gaze up at the moon, wondering what it would be like to actually walk on its surface. The moon had been full when she had arrived at camp on June 29. She had looked at it each night and watched it wane, growing smaller and smaller, sliver by sliver. The moon was almost fully cut in half, but it shone brilliantly bright on July 19 as she sat on her rock near the campfire looking up at it.

How she longed for news of the space mission! How were the astronauts doing? She knew it was almost 240,000 miles to the moon. Were they nearly there? There were no radios or TVs allowed at camp. She wished she could find a way to hear what was happening!

At last the campfire died down for the night. The singing and stories ended. It was time for the girls to head back to their cabins. Cathy was on her way to the bathrooms to wash up for bed when she heard a strange crackling noise, like static.

Cathy pushed aside the bushes along the dirt path. A girl her own age sat cross-legged on the ground. In the darkness, Cathy wasn't sure if she recognized this girl. The girl held a bright red metal box in one hand. She thumped the box with her other hand; then she adjusted the dial, trying to tune it in. The girl was so intent on what she was doing that she didn't even notice Cathy staring at her.

After a moment, the static sound stopped. Cathy heard a reporter's voice. The girl was listening to the news on a transistor radio!

"Cool!" Cathy whispered. The girl looked up sharply, seeing Cathy for the first time. She seemed alarmed that someone had discovered her.

"Did they walk on the moon yet?" Cathy asked her.

"I don't think so, not yet," the girl reported, with a sigh of relief. "I'm not supposed to have this in camp, so I keep it real low. But that makes it hard to hear."

The girl said her name was Carol. Cathy introduced herself. Cathy now realized that she had seen Carol before swimming in the lake and laughing with her friends at the lunch table next to hers. But, of course, they had never spoken.

From Carol's radio, Cathy learned that the Apollo 11 spacecraft was circling the moon. "The command ship will keep orbiting," Carol said. "Tomorrow, Michael Collins will stay in the command ship while Buzz Aldrin and Neil Armstrong go down to the moon's surface in a lunar module."

"When will they get out of the module?" Cathy breathed excitedly.

Carol put the radio close to her ear. "I don't think they're saying when."

Suddenly, a third girl joined them. "Are you listening to the Moon landing?" she asked excitedly.

"Quiet, Sue!" said Carol. "You know we're not supposed to have radios in camp. I don't want any of the counselors to hear it."

Sue lowered her voice to a murmur. "Did they walk on the moon yet?" she mumbled.

"Carol doesn't think so. They're still in orbit," Cathy told Sue. "I'm Cathy, by the way." Cathy realized that the words just came out, that she had introduced herself without even feeling stupid or shy.

Sue smiled broadly. "Hi, Cathy. I'm Sue. I think I've seen you at the lake or someplace. Isn't this the most exciting thing? I heard they're going to show the landing on TV. My mother wrote to tell me."

"I can't believe we're going to miss it!" Cathy said.

"I know!" Sue agreed wistfully. "I wish we were near a TV."

Suddenly a flashlight shone around them. "Do I hear a radio?" a counselor asked.

Carol snapped it off. "No, it's just us talking," Carol called back. "We're headed for the bathroom."

"Then get going," said the counselor.

"OK. We're going," Carol assured the counselor. She nodded to Sue and Cathy, and said, "Come on." And they jogged back to their cabins.

The next morning, July 20, Carol waved to Cathy at breakfast and motioned for Cathy to sit next to her. Carol introduced her to some girls from her cabin. Sue joined them with another girl named Liz. They all ate pancakes together while they talked excitedly about the upcoming Moon walk.

The girls were as excited as she was about the Moon walk. Cathy realized that she felt at ease with these girls. She didn't worry about saying something stupid or not having something to say. She had so many things in common with them that they found themselves talking incessantly to each other all morning. It was as if she had always known them. Periodically, during their excited chatter, when Cathy paused to listen to her new friends, she couldn't help but think how lucky she was to have found these friendships.

As they were finishing breakfast, Mrs. Moore, the head counselor, announced that there would be canoe races that day. They were to split into teams of three people to a canoe. "Want to be with Sue and me?" Carol invited Cathy.

"I don't think so," Cathy declined. "I'm not a very fast paddler. I just learned last week."

"Aw, who cares?" said Sue. "I just learned how to paddle too. Who cares whether we win or not? We'll just have fun."

"What's the worst thing that can happen?" added Sue.

"OK, I guess then," agreed Cathy, still feeling a little uncertain.

The camp canoe races took up most of the day. Cathy, Carol, and Sue always seemed to be going the wrong way—or in circles. During one race, Cathy accidentally sprayed Sue with a giant splash from her paddle. Sue jumped up in surprise and tipped the canoe. All three of them went straight into the lake.

Cathy had never laughed so hard in her life! They scrambled back in the canoe, gasping for air – not from being underwater, but from laughing nonstop.

Sue, Cathy, and Carol came in last place in every single race, but Cathy felt like they'd won. She'd had one of the most fun days she could remember. "July 20, 1969, is one day I will surely never forget," Cathy said, still doubled up in laughter, as she dripped dry.

"Neither will I!" agreed Sue.

"I know what you mean!" chimed in Carol.

Just then, Mrs. Moore headed toward them looking serious. The girls stopped smiling. She had Carol's little radio in her hand. "Carol, is this yours? It was left on your chair after breakfast," she said.

Carol nodded solemnly. "Yes, it's mine."

"You know radios are not allowed at camp. I'll have to take it from you."

"Oh, please don't," Carol begged. "We need it to hear the Moon landing! It should be soon – you can take it after!"

"Actually, the lunar module *Eagle* landed ten minutes ago at four-seventeen," Mrs. Moore told her.

Cathy gasped sharply, thrilled, and yet horrified that she had missed it. This was the first time people had landed on the moon—ever! "Did they get out of the module yet?" she interrupted.

"No, they won't leave for quite some time yet," Mrs. Moore replied.

"Oh, please, can we have the radio back, just for tonight?" Carol pleaded.

"No, Carol, I can't allow that. You know you weren't supposed to have it in the first place. Rules are rules. But because I understand why you brought it, there won't be any discipline other than the confiscation of your radio. I'll return it when camp ends," said Mrs. Moore as she left.

"This is terrible," wailed Sue. "A person will walk on the face of the moon for the first time in human history, and we won't get to see it!"

"We won't even get to hear it," Carol said tightly. She thumped herself lightly on the head. "How could I have been so stupid to leave my radio behind?!"

"It's all right, Carol," Cathy said, patting her new friend's shoulder. "Anyone could have made that mistake. We were all excited about the canoe race. You just weren't thinking about the radio then."

"I guess you're right. Thanks," sighed Carol.

That night after supper the campers had free time. This was unusual because most evenings there was some sort of activity planned. Cathy, Sue, Carol, Liz, and a few other girls sat down by the dock.

It wasn't fully dark, but the half moon had appeared, faint in the sky. "Do you think they'll find Moon people up there?" Cathy asked.

"I sure hope so," said Carol.

Liz wondered, "Do you think they'll find the man in the moon?" The girls laughed.

"What if the moon is really made of cheese and the landing module sinks in?" Sue suggested with a giggle.

"Well, then the astronauts will have plenty to eat!" joked Cathy.

The girls laughed and talked for another hour, looking up at the moon. It was dark, and the moon shone brightly down on the lake. Everything about the day had been wonderful, but none of the girls could help but think about how they had come so close to hearing the exciting historical Moon walk take place. Eventually, each girl stopped talking as they gazed at the stars and moon, and their minds wandered to the events taking place in space at the very location where they were staring.

Cathy heard footsteps approaching the dock and turned to see Mrs. Moore come down and talk to one of the waterfront counselors with a serious expression on her face. Was something wrong? She worried that it had to do with the Moon landing. Had there been an accident in space? Were the brave astronauts okay?

The waterfront counselor blew her whistle. "Everyone up to the main lodge, please. Right now!"

When Cathy and her new friends arrived at the camp's main lodge, all the campers were assembled on the porch. A television set had been placed by the front door. There was another set to the right and one to the left.

"Campers, tonight something quite thrilling will happen. We think it's important that you all see it, so settle in near one of the sets," explained Mrs. Moore.

Cathy couldn't believe it! She would get to see the walk after all! Her mouth broke into a huge grin, and it was contagious. Her friends' faces all beamed as well, and a second later they all burst into delighted giggles.

Cathy sat down beside Carol, Sue, and Liz as they settled near the right-hand television. On the screen was mission control on Earth. Men sat in front of monitors and machines full of dials. They were monitoring everything about the Moon mission. They learned that *Eagle* had landed on the part of the moon called the Sea of Tranquility. "Are they in water?" Liz asked.

"No," Cathy told her. "There's no water on the moon. It's called a sea because from Earth it appears smoother than other parts of the moon—kind of like our oceans look from space.

"What's 'tranquility'?" Carol asked.

"Quiet…calm," Cathy said. She remembered her mother saying she needed some tranquility after a busy day. "I guess they picked a calm place to land," Cathy said.

It was boring for a long time, but finally a grainy, black-and-white picture came on the screen. However, there was no doubt that the jumpy picture showed the surface of the moon.

In the next minute, Neil Armstrong and Buzz Aldrin stepped out of *Eagle* in their bulky space suits. They walked on the Moon in slow, bouncing steps. They planted an American flag and took pictures.

Carol squeezed Cathy's wrist. "This is so unbelievable!" she said in a low, thrilled whisper. "We'll always remember that we were here together at camp when they walked on the moon."

Cathy nodded. "We will," she agreed. Cathy suddenly realized that she felt very happy she had come to Camp Shining Lake. She was so glad she had made wonderful new friends who shared her excitement about the Moon walk. In fact, she was

already planning how they would write to each other during year, and maybe even get to visit each other during the winter. Then they would plan to return to camp the following summer.

Cathy would never forget this day—not the canoe race, not the Moon walk. She was beginning to think that maybe she could understand just a little of how the astronauts felt as they took their first steps in unfamiliar territory. In fact, while the astronauts explored a new world in outer space, Cathy had found a new world of friendship right here on Earth.

The Apollo 11 Moon Landing

The Apollo 11 mission launched on July 16, 1969. It carried Astronauts Neil Armstrong, Michael Collins, and Edwin Eugene "Buzz" Aldrin. On July 20, 1969, Buzz Aldrin and Neil Armstrong became the first people to land on the moon in the module *Eagle*. Michael Collins stayed behind, orbiting in the command module, *Columbia*.

Aldrin and Armstrong planted a flag on the moon and collected samples of the moon's surface, while people on Earth watched on TV. Almost anyone who is old enough to remember can tell you exactly where he or she was that night.

The astronauts left behind a golden olive branch to symbolize their peaceful intent and a plaque with this message: "Here men from the planet Earth first set foot upon the moon. We came in peace for all mankind."